Set design by Sandra Goldmark

Photo by Monique Carboni

Armando Riesco in the Page 73 Productions premiere of *Elliot, A Soldier's Fugue* at The Culture Project.

ELLIOT, A SOLDIER'S FUGUE

BY QUIARA ALEGRÍA HUDES

DRAMATISTS
PLAY SERVICE
INC.

ELLIOT, A SOLDIER'S FUGUE
Copyright © 2007, Quiara Alegría Hudes

All Rights Reserved

SPECIAL NOTE

Anyone receiving permission to produce ELLIOT, A SOLDIER'S FUGUE is required to give credit to the Author as sole and exclusive Author of the Play on the title page of all programs distributed in connection with performances of the Play and in all instances in which the title of the Play appears for purposes of advertising, publicizing or otherwise exploiting the Play and/or a production thereof. The name of the Author must appear on a separate line, in which no other name appears, immediately beneath the title and in size of type equal to 50% of the size of the largest, most prominent letter used for the title of the Play. No person, firm or entity may receive credit larger or more prominent than that accorded the Author. The following acknowledgment must appear on the title page in all programs distributed in connection with performances of the Play:

Original production produced by Page Seventy-Three Productions Inc.

SPECIAL NOTE ON SONGS AND RECORDINGS

For performances of copyrighted songs, arrangements or recordings mentioned in this Play, the permission of the copyright owner(s) must be obtained. Other songs, arrangements or recordings may be substituted provided permission from the copyright owner(s) of such songs, arrangements or recordings is obtained; or songs, arrangements or recordings in the public domain may be substituted.

For Elliot, Ginny and George.

With special thanks to Ray, Paula, and mom.

ELLIOT, A SOLDIER'S FUGUE was premiered by Page 73 Productions (Liz Jones, Asher Richelli, Nicole Fiz and Daniel Schiffman, Artistic Directors) at the Culture Project in New York City, opening on January 4, 2006. It was directed by Davis McCallum; the set design was by Sandra Goldmark; the costume design was by Chloe Chapin; the lighting design was by Joel Moritz; and the original music was by Michael Freedman. The cast was as follows:

ELLIOT .... Armando Riesco
GINNY .... Zabryna Guevara
POP .... Triney Sandoval
GRANDPOP .... Mateo Gómez

An early version of ELLIOT, A SOLDIER'S FUGUE was produced at Miracle Theatre in Portland, Oregon, in September 2005, directed by Olga Sanchez.

CHARACTERS

ELLIOT — serving in Iraq, 1st Marine Division, 19

POP — Elliot's father, served in Vietnam, 3rd Cavalry Division, various ages

GRANDPOP — Elliot's grandfather, served in Korea, 65th Infantry Regiment of Puerto Rico, various ages

GINNY — Elliot's mother, served in Vietnam, Army Nurse Corps, various ages

Sportscaster Voice, Producer Voice, and Radio Voice are to be distributed amongst the cast. Do not use prerecorded voices or add cast members.

SETTING

The set has two playing areas. The "empty space" is minimal, it transforms into many locations. It is stark, sad. When light enters, it is like light through a jailhouse window or through the dusty stained glass of a decrepit chapel. The "garden space," by contrast, is teeming with life. It is a verdant sanctuary, green speckled with magenta and gold. Both spaces are holy in their own way.

PRODUCTION NOTES

FUGUES

In the "fugue" scenes, people narrate each other's actions and sometimes narrate their own. For instance:

ELLIOT. A boy enters. *(Elliot enters.)*
GRANDPOP.
    Clean, deodorized.
    Some drops of water plummet from his nose and lips.
    The shower was ice cold.
(Elliot shivers.)

Elliot's action should mirror what the narrator, Grandpop, says. The narrator steps in and out of the scene as necessary.

POP'S LETTERS

Pop's letters are active and alive. They are not reflective, past-tense documents. They are immediate communication. Sometimes the letters are shared dialogue between Pop and Grandpop, but it should always be clear that it is Pop's story being spoken.

MUSIC

Flute. Bach, danzónes, jazz, etudes, scales, hip-hop beats. Overlapping lines.

OTHER

Please do not use actual barbed wire or vines in the wrapping scenes. The stage directions in these moments are an important part of the soul of the piece, but should not be staged literally.

ELLIOT, A SOLDIER'S FUGUE

1/FUGUE

The empty space, very empty. A pair of white underwear is on the ground. That's all we see.

GINNY.
A room made of cinderblock.
A mattress lies on a cot containing thirty-six springs.
If you lie on the mattress, you can feel each of the thirty-six springs.
One at a time.
As you close your eyes.
And try to sleep the full four hours.
POP.
A white sheet is on the mattress.
The corners are folded and tucked under.
Tight, like an envelope.
GRANDPOP.
Military code.
The corner of the sheet is checked at 0600 hours, daily.
No wrinkles or bumps allowed.
ELLIOT. A man enters. *(Elliot enters in a towel. It's 2003. He's eighteen.)*
GRANDPOP.
Clean, deodorized.
Some drops of water plummet from his nose and lips.
The shower was ice cold.
(Elliot shivers. He picks up the underwear.)
GINNY. He performs his own military-style inspection. *(Elliot*

*looks at the front and back of the underwear. No apparent stains. He
sniffs them. They're clean.)*
ELLIOT. Nice. *(Elliot puts them on under the towel, removes the towel.)*
POP.
> There's little bumps of skin on his arm.
> His pores tighten.
> His leg hair stands on end.
> Cold shower spray.
*(Elliot drops to the ground and does ten push-ups. He springs to his feet
and seems invigorated.)*
ELLIOT. One two three four five six seven eight nine ten. Rah!
POP. The mirror in the room reflects a slight distortion. *(Elliot
peers into the mirror — the audience.)*
GINNY.
> The chin.
> The teeth.
> Uppers and lowers.
> The molars.
> The one, lone filling.
*(He clenches his jaw, furrows his eyebrows. Holding the face, he curls a
bicep, showing off a round muscle.)*
ELLIOT. *(To the mirror adversary.)* What? You want to step? You're
making Subway hoagies. I'm a marine. Who are you? *(He shakes out
that pose. Now, he smiles like a little angel into the mirror. To the mirror mommy:)* Mami, quiero chuletas. Pasteles. Morsilla. Barbecue
ribs. Sorullito. Macaroni salad. Sopa de fideo. When I make it back
home, you gonna make me a plate, right? A montón of ribs. But no
pigs feet. Ain't no other Puerto Rican on this earth be cookin no pigs
feet. *(Elliot shakes out that pose. He leans in, an inch away from the
mirror. He pops a pimple. He wipes it on his underwear. He scrutinizes
his face for more pimples. There are none. He fixes his nearly-shaved hair.
He stands in a suave posture, leaning sexy. He blows a subtle kiss to the
mirror.)* You know you like it. Navy nursee want mi culito? *(He turns
around, looks at his butt in the mirror. He clenches his butt muscles and
releases. Then he does this about ten times in a quick succession, watching the mirror the whole time. He stops.)*
POP.
> Blank.
> He's nervous about something.
GRANDPOP. He will board the ship to Iraq at 0700 hours. *(Elliot
starts to put on his uniform under … The room is empty. A towel is on*

the floor.)
GINNY.

> A room with steel doors.
> Steel walls, steel windows.
> The room sways up and down.
> Hammocks on top of hammocks swing back and forth.

GRANDPOP.

> The room is inside a boat.
> That's on the ocean to Vietnam.

GINNY. The floors of the USS Eltinge are inspected at 0530 daily.
POP and GRANDPOP.

> Military code.
> No dirt allowed.

GINNY.

> But the floor is wet.
> It's the Pacific Ocean, seeping inside.

POP. A young man enters. *(Pop enters. It's 1966. He wears a uniform and catches his breath.)*
GINNY.

> The 0400 deck run was hot.
> The shower will be warm.
> Six hundred and forty muscles will relax.

GRANDPOP.

> Military code.
> No bare chests.

(Pop untucks his shirt, unbuttons it, throws it to the floor.)
POP. *(Imitating a drill sergeant under his breath. Faux southern accent.)*
Keep up the pace, Ortiz. You can't hear me, Ortiz? Are you deaf, Ortiz? Corporal Feifer, is Corporal Ortiz deaf?
GRANDPOP.

> Military code.
> No bare feet.

(He takes off his boots, peels off his socks.)
POP. You're the best damn shot in the marines, Ortiz. You could kill a fly. Does your momma know what a great shot you are?
GINNY. Reflect honor upon yourself and your home country. *(He peels off his undershirt.)*
POP. Where are you from, Ortiz? What's your momma's name? Eh? Is she fat like you? Your momma got a fat ass, Ortiz? *(Elliot is fully dressed. He salutes the mirror.)*
ELLIOT. Lance Corporal Elliot Ortiz Third Light Armored Recon

Battalion First Marine Division. Mutha fucka. *(Pop finds a paper and pencil. He taps the pencil, thinking of what to write. Elliot checks inside his duffel bag.)*

GINNY.

    The duffel is heavy full of boots and pants.

    A map of Iraq.

    A Bible with four small photographs.

GRANDPOP.

    Military code.

    No electronic devices.

ELLIOT. Got my walkman.

GRANDPOP.

    Military code.

    No valuables.

ELLIOT. My Nas CD. Jay Z. Slow Jams. Reggaetón 2002.

POP. April 12, 1966 … *(Elliot opens a little green Bible, looks at photos.)*

ELLIOT. My photos. Mom. In your garden. *(He kisses the photo. Finds a new one.)* Grandpop. Senile old head. *(Taps the photo. Finds a new one.)* Pops. With your beer-ass belly.

POP. *(Writing.)* Dear pop …

ELLIOT. *(Still to the photo.)* When I get home, we gonna have a father and son. Chill in mom's garden. Drink some bud light out them mini cans. I don't want to hear about no "leave the past in the past." You gonna tell me your stories. *(Elliot puts on headphones and starts bobbing his head to the hip-hop beat. Pop continues to write under … The room is empty. A towel is on the floor.)*

GINNY.

    A tent.

    No windows, no door.

    Walls made of canvas.

    A floor made of dirt.

    The soil of Inchon, Korea is frozen.

GRANDPOP.

    Sixteen cots they built by hand.

    Underwear, towels, unmade beds.

    Dirty photos.

GINNY.

    That is, snapshots of moms and daughters and wives

    That have dirt on them.

GRANDPOP. A boy enters. *(Grandpop enters. It's 1950. He's wear-*

ing heavy soldier clothes. He rubs his arms for warmth. He puts on additional clothing layers.)
GINNY.
　　His breath crystallizes.
　　His boots are full of icy sweat.
　　The 0500 swamp run was subzero.
(Grandpop blows into his hands for warmth. He bends his fingers.)
GRANDPOP. One two three four ... five. My thumb is as purple as a flower. *(He pulls a black leather case from his cot. He opens it, revealing a flute. He pulls out pieces of the flute, begins to assemble them, cleaning dirt from the joints.)* Ah, this Korean dirt is too damn dirty. We lost another man to frostbite this week. These guys deserve some Bach. Light as a feather,
POP. *(Finishing the letter.)* Your son,
GRANDPOP. free as a bird.
POP. Little George.
(Grandpop puts the flute to his lips, inhales, begins to play. The melody of a Bach passacaglia. Pop folds up the letter, puts it in an envelope. Addresses the envelope.)
GINNY.
　　Military code.
　　Make no demands.
　　Military code.
　　Treat women with respect.
　　Military code.
　　Become friends with fellow soldiers.
　　No rude behavior.
　　Pray in silence, please.
(Pop drops the letter, lays down, sings himself to sleep. It overlaps with Grandpop's flute and Elliot's head-bobbing. Based on traditional military cadences:)
POP.
　　One, two, three, four
　　We're gonna jump on the count of four
　　If I die when I hit the mud
　　Bury me with a case of bud
　　A case of bud and a bottle of rum
　　Drunk as hell in kingdom come
　　Count off
　　One, two, three, four.
(Elliot skips forward a few tracks on the walkman, finds his jam. Head

bobbing, he marks the beat, sings along an occasional lyric as he is
inspired to. He is listening to a song like Nas' "Got Urself a Gun" or
another rap song from 2001, at maximum headphone volume.* His
beat synchs up with Pop.)
ELLIOT.
Unh, unh.
Unh, unh.

	POP.
	One, two, three, four
	We're gonna charge on the count of four
Unh, unh.	If my heart begins to bleed
	Bury me with a bag full a' weed
Unh, unh.	A bag full a' weed and a
	Bottle of rum
Unh, unh.	Laugh at the devil in kingdom come
	Count off
Unh, unh, unh, unh.	Bud bud bud bud
Unh, unh.	Bud bud bud bud

(It is three-part counterpoint between the men. Lights fade, counter-
point lingers.)

2/PRELUDE

The empty space. A flashbulb goes off.

SPORTSCASTER VOICE. Thanks, Harry. I'm standing outside
the Phillies locker room with hometown hero Lance Corporal
Elliot Ortiz. He'll be throwing out tonight's opening pitch.
ELLIOT. Call me Big El.
SPORTSCASTER VOICE. You were one of the first marines to
cross into Iraq.
ELLIOT. Two days after my eighteenth birthday.
SPORTSCASTER VOICE. And you received a Purple Heart at
19. Big El, welcome home.
ELLIOT. *Philly!*

---

* See Special Note on Songs and Recordings on copyright page.

SPORTSCASTER VOICE. You're in Philadelphia for a week and then it's back to Iraq for your second tour of duty?

ELLIOT. We'll see. I got until Friday to make up my mind.

SPORTSCASTER VOICE. Did you miss the city of brotherly love?

ELLIOT. Mom's food. My girl Stephanie. My little baby cousin. Cheese steaks.

SPORTSCASTER VOICE. Any big plans while you're home?

ELLIOT. Basically eat. Do some interviews. My mom's gonna fix up my leg. I'm a take my pop out for a drink, be like, alright, old head. Time to trade some war stories.

SPORTSCASTER VOICE. I hope you order a Shirley temple. Aren't you nineteen?

ELLIOT. I'll order a Shirley temple.

SPORTSCASTER VOICE. Big Phillies fan?

ELLIOT. Three years in a row I was Lenny Dykstra for Halloween.

SPORTSCASTER VOICE. A few more seconds to pitch time.

ELLIOT. Hold up. Quick shout out to North Philly. Second and Berks, share the love! To my moms. My pops. I'm doing it for you. Grandpops — videotape this so you don't forget! Stephanie. All my friends still out there in Iraq. Waikiki, one of these days I'm going to get on a plane to Hawaii and your mom better cook me some Kahlua pig.

SPORTSCASTER VOICE. Curve ball, fast ball?

ELLIOT. Wait and see. I gotta keep you on your toes. I'm gonna stand on that mound and show ya'll I got an arm better than Schilling! Record lightning speed!

3/PRELUDE

The garden. Grandpop opens a letter and reads. Pop appears separately.

GRANDPOP and POP. May 24, 1966
POP.
 Dear pop,
  It's hot wet
GRANDPOP. cold muddy

POP. miserable. Operation Prairie has us in the jungle, and it's a sauna.

GRANDPOP. One hundred twenty degrees by 1100 hours,

POP. you think you're gonna cook by 1300. Then yesterday it starts to rain.

GRANDPOP. Drops the size of marbles —

POP. my first real shower in weeks. Monsoon. They said,

GRANDPOP. "Get used to it." Corporal shoved a machete in my hand and told me to lead.

POP. He's the leader, but I get to go first!

GRANDPOP. I cut through the vines, clear the way. We get lesions,

POP. ticks,

GRANDPOP. leeches.

POP. At night we strip down, everybody pulls the things off each other. We see a lot of rock ape.

GRANDPOP. They're bigger than chimps and they throw rocks at us.

POP. They've got great aim! You just shoot up in the air, they run away.

GRANDPOP. At night you can't see your own hand in front of your face.

POP. I imagine you and mom on the back stoop, having a beer. Uncle Tony playing his guitar. My buddy Joe Bobb,

GRANDPOP. from Kentucky.

POP. He carries all his equipment on his back, plus a guitar, and he starts playing these hillbilly songs.

GRANDPOP. They're pretty good.

POP. I think Uncle Tony would like them. I pulled out your flute and we jammed a little. C-rations, gotta split,

POP and GRANDPOP. Little George.

4/PRELUDE

Ginny in the garden.

GINNY. The garden is twenty-five years old. It used to be abandoned. There was glass everywhere. Right here, it was a stripped-down school bus. Here, a big big pile of old tires. I bought it for one dollar. A pretty good deal. Only a few months after I came back from Vietnam. I told myself, you've got to *do* something. So I bought it. I went and got a ton of dirt from Sears. Dirt is expensive! I said, when I'm done with this, it's going to be a spitting image of Puerto Rico. Of Arecibo. It's pretty close. You can see electric wires dangling like right there and there. But I call that "native Philadelphia vines." If you look real close, through the heliconia you see anti-theft bars on my window.

Green things, you let them grow wild. Don't try to control them. Like people, listen to them, let them do their own thing. You give them a little guidance on the way. My father was a mean bastard. The first time I remember him touching me, it was to whack me with a shoe. He used to whack my head with a wooden spoon every time I cursed. I still have a bump on my head from that. Ooh, I hated him. But I was mesmerized to see him with his plants. He became a saint if you put a flower in his hand. Secrets, when things grow at night. Phases of the moon. He didn't need a computer, he had it all in his brain. "I got no use for that." That was his thing. "I got no use for church." "I got no use for a phone." "I got no use for children." He had use for a flower.

There are certain plants you only plant at night. Orchids. Plants with provocative shapes. Plants you want to touch. Sexy plants. My garden is so sexy. If I was young, I'd bring all the guys here. The weirdest things get my juices going. I sit out here at night, imagine romances in the spaces between banana leaves. See myself as a teenager, in Puerto Rico, a whole different body on these bones. I'm with a boyfriend, covered in dirt.

When I was a nurse in the Army Nurse Corps, they brought men in by the loads. The evacuation hospital. The things you see. Scratched corneas all the way to. A guy with the back of his body torn off. You get the man on the cot, he's screaming. There's men screaming all around. Always the same thing, calling out for his mother, his wife, girlfriend. First thing, before anything else, I would make eye contact. I always looked them in the eye, like to say, hey, it's just you and me. Touch his face like I was his wife. Don't look at his wound, look at him like he's the man of my dreams. Just for one tiny second. Then, it's down to business. Try to keep that heart going, that breath pumping in and out, keep that blood inside the tissue. Sometimes I was very attracted to the men I worked on. A tenderness would sweep through me. Right before dying, your body goes into shock. Pretty much a serious case of the shakes. If I saw a man like that, I thought, would he like one last kiss? One last hand on his ass? Give him a good going away party.

Just things in my mind. Not things you act on.

With George, though. We had a great time when he was in the evacuation hospital. I stitched his leg up like a quilt and we stayed up all night smoking joints. Everyone in the hospital was passed out asleep. The first time George got up and walked to me. I took his head in my right hand and I kissed him so hard. That kiss was the best feeling in my body. Ooh. You see so much death, then someone's lips touches yours and you go on vacation for one small second.

Gardening is like boxing. It's like those days in Vietnam. The wins versus the losses. Ninety percent of it is failures but the triumphs? When Elliot left for Iraq, I went crazy with the planting. Begonias, ferns, trees. A seed is a contract with the future. It's saying, I know something better will happen tomorrow. I planted bearded irises next to palms. I planted tulips with a border of cacti. All the things the book tells you, "Don't ever plant these together." "Guide to Proper Gardening." Well I got on my knees and planted them side by side. I'm like, you have to throw all preconceived notions out the window. You have to plant wild. When your son goes to war, you plant every goddam seed you can find. It doesn't matter what the seed is. So long as it grows. I plant like I want and to hell with the consequences. I planted a hundred clematis vines by the kitchen window, and next thing I know sage is growing there. The tomato vines gave me beautiful tomatoes. The bamboo shot out from the ground. And the heliconia! *(She retrieves a heliconia leaf.)* Each leaf is actually a cup. It collects the rainwater. So any weary traveler can stop and take a drink.

5/PRELUDE

The garden. Grandpop opens a letter and reads. Pop appears separately.

POP. October 7, 1966
GRANDPOP. Dear dad and all the rest of you lucky people,

POP. Got my next assignment. All those weeks of waiting and boredom? Those are the good old days! They marched us to Dong Ha for Operation Prairie 2. I'm infantry. Some guys drive, go by tank. Infantry walks. We walk by the side of the tank. Two days straight, we've been scouting for body parts. You collect what you find, throw it in the tank, they label it and take it away. Where they take it? You got me. What they write on the label? It's like bird watching. You develop your eye.

GRANDPOP. Don't show this letter to mom, please. And don't ask me about it when I get home. If I feel like talking about it I will but otherwise don't ask.

POP. Today this one little shrimp kept hanging around, chasing after the tank. Looking at me with these eyes. I gave him my crackers I was saving for dinner. I made funny faces and he called me dinky dow. That's Vietnamese for crazy, I guess. Dinky dow! Dinky dow! He inhaled those crackers then he smiled and hugged my leg. He was so small he only came up to my knee.

6/FUGUE

The empty space. Two wallets are on the ground.

GINNY.
    In my dreams, he said.
    Everything is in green.
    Green from the night vision goggles.
    Green Iraq.
    Verdant Falluja.
    Emerald Tikrit.
(Elliot enters. He puts on night vision goggles.)
ELLIOT. *(To imaginary night patrol partner.)* Waikiki man, whatchu gonna eat first thing when you get home? I don't know. Probably start me off with some French toast from Denny's. Don't even get me near the cereal aisle. I'll go crazy. I yearn for some cereal. If you had to choose between Cocoa Puffs and Count Chocula, what would you choose? Wheaties or Life? Fruity Pebbles or Crunchberry? You know my mom don't even buy Cap'n Crunch. She buys King

Vitaman. Cereal so cheap, it don't even come in a box. It comes in a bag like them cheap Jewish noodles.

GINNY. Nightmares every night, he said.

A dream about the first guy he actually saw that he killed.

A dream that doesn't let you forget a face.

ELLIOT. The ultimate Denny's challenge. Would you go for the Grand Slam or the French Toast Combo? Wait. Or Western Eggs with Hash Browns? Yo, hash browns with ketchup. Condiments. Mustard, tartar sauce. I need me some condiments.

GINNY.

> Green moon.
>
> Green star.
>
> Green blink of the eye.
>
> Green teeth.
>
> The same thing plays over and over.

(Elliot's attention is suddenly distracted.)

ELLIOT. Yo, you see that?

GINNY. The green profile of a machine gun in the distance.

ELLIOT. Waikiki, look straight ahead. Straight, at that busted wall. Shit. You see that guy? What's in his hand? He's got an AK. What do you mean, "I don't know." Do you see him? *(Elliot looks out.)* We got some hostiles. Permission to shoot. *(Pause.)* Permission to open fire. *(Pause.)* Is this your first? Shit, this is my first, too. Alright. You ready?

GINNY.

> In the dream, aiming in.
>
> In the dream, knowing his aim is exact.
>
> In the dream, closing his eyes.

(Elliot closes his eyes.)

ELLIOT. Bang. *(Elliot opens his eyes.)*

GINNY.

> Opening his eyes.
>
> The man is on the ground.

ELLIOT. Hostile down. Uh, target down. *(Elliot gets up, disoriented from adrenaline.)*

GINNY. In the dream, a sudden movement.

ELLIOT. Bang bang. Oh shit. That fucker moved. Did you see that? He moved, right? Mother f. Target down. Yes, I'm sure. Target down.

GINNY.

> Nightmares every night, he said.
>
> A dream about the first guy he actually saw that he killed.

(Pop enters, sits on the ground. He's trying to stay awake. He looks

through binoculars.)

GRANDPOP. In my dreams, he said.

GINNY. Walking toward the guy. *(Elliot walks to the wallet.)*

GRANDPOP. Everything is a whisper.

GINNY. Standing over the guy. *(Elliot looks down at the wallet.)*

GRANDPOP. Breathing is delicate.

GINNY. A green face.

GRANDPOP. Whisper of water in the river.

GINNY. A green forehead.

GRANDPOP. Buzz of mosquito.

GINNY. A green upper lip.

GRANDPOP. Quiet Dong-Ha.

GINNY. A green river of blood. *(Elliot kneels down, reaches to the wallet on the ground before him. It represents the dead man. He puts his hand on the wallet and remains in that position.)*

GRANDPOP. Echo Vietnam.

POP. Joe Bobb. Wake up, man. Tell me about your gang from Kentucky. What, back in the Bronx? Yeah, we got ourselves a gang, but not a bad one. We help people on our street. Like some kids flipped over an ice cream stand. It was just a nice old guy, the kids flipped it, knocked the old guy flat. We chased after them. Dragged one. Punched him til he said sorry. We called ourselves the Social Sevens. After the Magnificent Sevens.

GRANDPOP.
　　　　Nightmares every night, he said.
　　　　A dream that doesn't let you forget a voice.
　　　　The same sounds echoing back and forth.

POP. Guns? Naw, we weren't into none of that. We threw a lot of rocks and bottles. And handballs. Bronx Handball Champs, 1964. Doubles and singles. Hm? What's a handball?

GRANDPOP. The snap of a branch.

POP. Shh.

GRANDPOP. Footsteps in the mud.

POP. You hear something?

GRANDPOP.
　　　　Three drops of water.
　　　　A little splash.

(Pop grabs his binoculars and looks out.)

POP. VC on us. Ten o'clock. Kneeling in front of the river, alone. He's drinking. Fuck, he's thirsty. Joe Bobb, man, this is my first time. Oh shit. Shit. Bang. *(Pause.)* Bang.

19

GRANDPOP.
>Whisper of two bullets in the air.
>Echo of his gun.
>A torso falling in the mud.

POP. Got him. I got him, Joe Bobb. Man down. VC down. *(Pop rises, looks out.)*

GRANDPOP.
>Hearing everything.
>Walking to the guy.
>Boots squishing in the mud.

(Pop walks to the second wallet.)
>Standing over the guy.
>The guy says the Vietnamese word for "mother."
>He has a soft voice.
>He swallows air.
>A brief convulsion.
>Gasp.
>Silence.
>Water whispers in the river.

POP and ELLIOT.
>Military code.
>Remove ID and intel from dead hostiles.

(Pop kneels in front of the wallet. It represents the dead man. He reaches out his hand and touches the wallet. Elliot and pop are in the same position, each of them touching a wallet. They move in unison.)

POP.
>The wallet
>The body
>The face
>The eyes

(Elliot and pop open the wallets.)

ELLIOT.
>The photo
>The pictures
>Bullet

(Elliot and pop each pull a little photo out of the wallets.)

POP.
>Dog tags
>The wife

ELLIOT.
>The children

(They turn over the photo and look at the back of it.)
    Black ink
POP. A date
POP and ELLIOT.
    Handwriting
    A family portrait
(They drop the photo. They find a second photo. Lights fade.)

7/PRELUDE

The empty space. A flash bulb goes off. Elliot is in a TV studio. Harsh studio lighting is on him.

PRODUCER VOICE. ABC evening local news. And we're rolling to tape in three, two …
ELLIOT. *(Tapping a mike on his shirt collar.)* Hello? What? Yeah. So where do we start? *(He presses his fingers against his ear, indicating that a producer or someone is talking to him through an ear monitor.)* My name? Elliot Ortiz. *(Listens.)* Sorry. Lance Corporal Elliot Ortiz, 3rd Light Armored Recon Battalion, 1st Marine Division. *(Listens.)* What? How was I injured?
PRODUCER VOICE. *(Impatient.)* Someone fix his monitor. Don't worry, Mr. uh, Ortiz. Just tell us the story of your injury, would you?
ELLIOT. Okay. Well. I was on watch outside Tikrit. I don't know. I feel stupid. I already told this story once.
PRODUCER VOICE. You did?
ELLIOT. Just now. In the screen test.
PRODUCER VOICE. Right, right. That was to acclimate you to the camera.
ELLIOT. It loses the impact to repeat it over and over.
PRODUCER VOICE. Was it scary?
ELLIOT. People say, oh that must be scary. But when you're there, you're like, oh shit, and you react. When it's happening you're not thinking about it. You're like, damn, this is really happening. That's all you can think. You're in shock basically. It's a mentality. Kill or be killed. You put everything away and your mentality is war. Some people get real gung ho about fighting. I was laid back.

PRODUCER VOICE. Yes, Mr. uh Ortiz. This is great. This is exactly it. Let's go back and do you mind repeating a couple sentences, same exact thing, without the expletives?

ELLIOT. Say what?

PRODUCER VOICE. Same thing. But no shit and no damn.

ELLIOT. I don't remember word for word.

PRODUCER VOICE. No problem. Here we go. "But when you're there, you're like, oh shit, and you react."

ELLIOT. But when you're there you're like, oh snap, and you react.

PRODUCER VOICE. "You're like, damn, this is really happening."

ELLIOT. You're like, flip, this is really happening.

PRODUCER VOICE. Flip? Do people say "flip" these days?

ELLIOT. You're like, FUCK, this is really happening.

PRODUCER VOICE. Cut!

ELLIOT. It's a marine thing.

8/PRELUDE

Grandpop in the garden.

GRANDPOP. Of everything Bach wrote, it is the fugues. The fugue is like an argument. It starts in one voice. The voice is the melody, the single solitary melodic line. The statement. Another voice creeps up on the first one. Voice two responds to voice one. They tangle together. They argue, they become messy. They create dissonance. Two, three, four lines clashing. You think, good god, they'll never untie themselves. How did this mess get started in the first place? Major keys, minor keys, all at once on top of each other. *(Leans in.)* It's about untying the knot.

In Korea my platoon fell in love with Bach. All night long, firing eight-inch howitzers into the evergreens. Flute is very soothing after the bombs settle down. They begged me to play. "Hey, Ortiz, pull out that pipe!" I taught them minor key versus major key. Minor key, it's melancholy, it's like the back of the woman you love as she walks away from you. Major key, well that's more simple, like how the sun rises. They understood. If we had a rough battle, if we lost one of our guys, they said, "Eh, Ortiz, I need a minor key." But if they had just got a letter from home, a note from the lady, then they want C major, up-tempo.

"Light as a feather, free as a bird." My teacher always said the same thing. Let your muscles relax. Feel like a balloon is holding up your spine. He was a gringo but he lived with us rural Puerto Ricans. Way in the mountains. He was touring in San Juan with his famous jazz combo, fell in love with a woman, never left. We accepted him as one of our own. He was honorary Boricua. "Light as a feather, free as a bird." I said, you know, if I get any lighter and freer, I'll float to the moon. But that's how you learn. By repeating. Over and over. At Inchon my right hand was purple with frostbite, I developed a technique for left-hand only. In Kunu-Ri? Every night we took our weapons to bed, like a wife. One night I shot myself in the shoulder. So I mastered the left-hand method.

Elliot always wanted to know. "Abuelo, tell me a story." About life in the service, about Puerto Rico. "Abuelo, how old were you when? How old were you when this, when that?" Carajo, I don't remember! All I know is what music I was playing at the time. When I started school, when I was a boy, helping mom in the house, it was etudes and scales. The foundations. The first girl I "danced with," it was danzónes around that time, mambo with a touch of jazz. But In Korea, I played Bach only. Because it is cold music, it is like math. You can approach it like a calculation. An exercise. A routine.

At the airport, I handed the flute to little George. I thought, he needs a word of advice, but what is there to say? I sent him to boot camp with a fifty dollar bill and a flute. That he didn't know how to play. But without it my fingers grew stiff. I started losing words. Dates. Names of objects. Family names. Battles I had fought in. I started repeating words as if I was playing scales. Practice. Bookmarks to remind myself. "Inchon, Inchon, Inchon." "Korea, Korea." "Bayamón." "Howitzer." "Evergreen."

9/PRELUDE

The garden. Grandpop opens a letter and reads. Pop appears separately, in a good mood.

POP.
>November 30, 1966
>Did you ever notice a helmet is an incredibly useful item? I got
>a wide range of artistic and practical uses for mine.

GRANDPOP. Today I took a bath, if you want to call it that, out of my helmet. The newer ones have two parts.

POP. If you take the metal part out, you can cook in it. Tonight we had two cans of tuna. A hamburger in gravy. Hess' contribution?

POP and GRANDPOP. Ham with lima beans.

POP. Everyone empties out their cans. Make a little blue campfire with some minor explosives. Voila,

GRANDPOP. Helmet stew.

POP.
>So that's our Thanksgiving feast. The guys are singing carols.
>   They're in the spirit!
>Jingle bells
>Mortar shells
>VC in the grass
>Take your Merry Christmas
>And shove it up your ass

10/FUGUE

The empty space. Two cots are there. Elliot lies on the ground. Grandpop, Ginny and Pop wrap Elliot's legs in barbed wire. They entangle Elliot in this position, trapping him. Elliot lies helpless.

GINNY.
>A road outside Tikrit.
>A mile short of Saddam's hometown.

GRANDPOP. Cars are allowed out, but not back in.

POP. The boy was standing guard.

GRANDPOP. He saw an incoming car.

GINNY. The headlights approached.

POP. He fired into the car.

GRANDPOP. The horn sounded.

POP. The car collided into the barricade.

GINNY. The concertina wire slinkied onto his legs.

GRANDPOP. Two seconds ago.

ELLIOT. Sarge! Sarge! Waikiki!

GINNY. Seventy four thorns dig deep into his skin.

POP. Seventy four barbs chew into his bone.

GRANDPOP. It is not a sensation of rawness.

GINNY. It is not excruciating pain.

POP. It is a penetrating weakness.

GRANDPOP. Energy pours out of his leg.

GINNY. Like water from a garden hose.

ELLIOT. Sarge!

POP. The boy knows he is trapped.

GRANDPOP. He doesn't know he is injured.

GINNY. He does a military style inspection. *(Elliot reaches up his pants leg.)*

GRANDPOP. His hand enters the warm meat of his calf.

ELLIOT. Oh shit. Stay calm. Put the tourniquet on. Lay back. Drink a cup of water. *(Elliot pulls a strip of cloth from his pocket. He wraps it like a tourniquet around his thigh. Tight.)*

GINNY. Forty-one percent of all injuries are leg wounds.

POP. Military code.

GRANDPOP. Carry a tourniquet at all times.

GINNY. Instructions in the event of rapid blood loss.

GRANDPOP. One.

ELLIOT. Stay calm.

POP. Two.

ELLIOT. Put the tourniquet on.

GRANDPOP. Three.

ELLIOT.
    Lay back.
    Four ... Four?

GINNY. Drink a cup of water.

ELLIOT. Someone get me a cup of water.

POP. Stay

GRANDPOP.
    Calm
    Put

POP. Tourniquet

GINNY. Lay

GRANDPOP.

Back
Drink
POP. Cup
GINNY. Water
ELLIOT. Hello? Stay calm. Put a beret on. Fall away. Drink a hot tub. Fuck. Stay with me, Ortiz. Big El going to be okay. Hello? Big El okay. Right?
POP. Fast forward pictures.
GINNY. Mom
POP. Pop
GRANDPOP. Grandpop
POP. Fast forward.
GINNY. Grandpop
GRANDPOP. Pop
POP. Mom
GINNY. Rapid shutter motion.
GRANDPOP. Frames with no sound.
GINNY. Moving lips, no words.
ELLIOT. Mom
POP. Pop
GRANDPOP. Grandpop
ELLIOT. Stay calm. Lay back. Smoke a cigarette. *(He pulls a cigarette out of his pocket.)* Anyone got a light? *(He smokes the unlit cigarette.)*
POP. Instructions if wounded while alone.
GRANDPOP. Call for help.
POP. Signal commander.
GINNY. Call for your corpsman.
POP. Identify yourself.
ELLIOT. Sarge! Waikiki! Big El down. Big El down.
POP. His blood congeals in the sand.
GRANDPOP. His fingertips are cool.
GINNY. He enters a euphoric state.
GRANDPOP. The boots,
ELLIOT. Beautiful.
POP. The barbed wire,
ELLIOT. Beautiful.
GINNY. The stars,
ELLIOT. Beautiful.
GINNY.

In the event of extended blood loss.

Reflect on a time you were happy.

When have you felt a sensation of joy?

ELLIOT.

Mom ...

Pop ...

(Elliot remains injured under ... Pop enters and lays on a cot.)

GRANDPOP.

An evacuation hospital.

Made of a Vietnamese monastery.

Ancient windows with no glass.

GINNY.

Through the window, views of Vietnam.

That look like views of Puerto Rico.

Mountains.

ELLIOT. Mountains.

GRANDPOP. Waterfalls.

ELLIOT. Waterfalls.

GINNY.

All different colors of green.

Rock formations.

A few bald spots from the bombs.

GRANDPOP.

The wood floor is covered with cement.

The cement is covered with water and blood.

The cement is cool.

The blood is cool.

ELLIOT. Cool. *(Elliot nods off, going into shock.)*

GINNY.

A woman enters.

(Ginny enters, approaches pop's cot.)

Hey.

POP. Nurse Ginny. Still on duty?

GINNY. Shh. Don't wake the babies.

POP. Can't sleep?

GINNY. Yeah.

POP. Me too.

GINNY. Nightmares. Weird stuff, I kept seeing your leg. I thought I should check up on you.

POP. It itches, but you know. The guy next to me's got no left leg at all.

GINNY. I was thinking, a private physical therapy session.

POP. Sounds good.

GINNY. Clean you up. *(Ginny lifts up his pant leg. There is a big gauze patch there. She slowly pulls back the gauze.)*
POP. That's as far back as it goes. The rest is stuck to the gauze.
GINNY. We're all out of anesthetic. I'll be gentle. *(She works on his wound. He is clearly in physical pain.)*

> Twenty eight stitches.
> Two diagonals.
> The first time she touched the man's wound,
> A pain pierced up through her index finger.
> Through her knuckle.
> Wrist.
> Forearm.
> Elbow.
> Humerus.
> Shoulder.
> The pain jolted in her veins.
> Exploded in her vital organs.
> Pancreas, lungs, brains, spleen.
> Planted itself between her legs.
> She touched the blood on his skin and had the desire to make love to the wounded man.

POP. Ay dios mio. Fuck.
GINNY. Think of the time in life you were happiest.
POP. Why?
GINNY. You forget the pain.
POP. It's not pain. It fucking itches!
GINNY. Sorry.
POP. Sorry. *(Pause. Ginny covers the wound. She pulls down his pant leg. She sits on top him.)*
GINNY. Is it too much weight?
POP. Please, crush me to death.
GINNY. There's too many bells and whistles in hospitals. To be a nurse is easy. Give a dog a bone.
POP. Reach into my pocket.
GINNY. Lance Corporal Ortiz.
POP. Go ahead. *(She puts her hand into his pocket. She feels around.)*
GINNY. What am I looking for?
POP. You'll know when you find it. *(She removes her hand from his pocket. She's holding a joint.)* Medicine.
GINNY. Anesthetic. *(Ginny lights the joint. They pass it back and forth. Between inhales, they touch each other.)*

GRANDPOP.

    Through the window, views of Vietnam.

    That look like views of Puerto Rico.

    Mountains.

    Green.

    Stars.

    Bamboo.

    Little huts up the mountainside.

POP. *(Stoned.)* I got one. I was a little boy in Puerto Rico. Bayamón. I had this ugly scrappy dog. We used to run around scaring my dad's roosters. One of the roosters got pissed and poked the dog's left eye out.

GINNY. What was his name?

POP. Jimmy.

GINNY. Jimmy? Jimmy! *(Elliot shivers.)*

ELLIOT. Ugghhh …

POP. Shh. Did you hear something? The operating room.

GINNY. No, it's the monkeys. There's a whole family of them that live in the tree.

POP. They're not rock ape are they?

GINNY. What's rock ape?

POP. Big, brown, and ugly.

GINNY. Rock ape! *(They laugh. She suddenly gets off of him and walks to a far corner of the room. She still has the joint.)* Tonight you're going to do like Jesus did. You're going to get up and walk on water. Defy all the odds. And I'm going to do like a circus tamer. Like someone who trains dogs or exotic animals. If you're a good tiger and you do your trick and you don't bite, you get a reward. If you do your dolphin tricks, I give you a fish.

POP. Seafood is my favorite.

GINNY. Walk to me. See if you can make it.

POP. Not even a hand out of bed?

GINNY. If you want a taste of this ripe avocado, you got to pick it off the tree all by yourself. *(Pop struggles to get up. This is a difficult, painful process. He slowly makes his way across the room.)*

POP.

Shrapnel.

In the ligaments.

In the soft-hard knee cap.

In the spaces between stitches.

Shrapnel from a mortar bomb.

ELLIOT.

Stay

Back

Splinters that fragment within you.   Lay
Wobbling within your guts.
Creating ripples in your bloodstream.   Home
(Pop arrives at Ginny. He falls into her. They kiss.)
ELLIOT. Signal
    Elliot Ortiz. *(Ginny and Pop stop kissing.)*
POP. Do you heal all your patients this way?
ELLIOT. Ortiz.
GINNY. Let's go outside and watch the monkeys.
POP. No, really. You do this a lot?
ELLIOT. Ortiz.
GINNY. Think you can make it outside?
POP. Give me a hand this time.
ELLIOT. Ortiz.
GINNY. There's a gorgeous view of the moon. *(They exit, slowly, carefully, in each other's arms. They pass in front of Elliot, who is shivering.)*
ELLIOT.
    Mom?
    Pop?

11/PRELUDE

The empty space. Elliot wears big radio station headphones.

RADIO VOICE. You're listening to WHYY, member supported radio, welcome back. I'm having a conversation with Elliot Ortiz, a North Philadelphia native who graduated from Edison High in 2002. So, Elliot, you're seventeen years old, just finishing boot camp, and the President declares war. What was going through your mind?
ELLIOT. I was like, okay then, let's do this.
RADIO VOICE. You were ready. Is it exciting to be a marine?
ELLIOT. People say, oh, it's like a video game. Oh, it's like the movies. Naw. Base is the most depressing place ever. You wake up, go outside, you see rocky sand mountains. That's it. Rocks. Sand. You gotta drive thirty minutes to find a Wal-Mart. I just mainly stay on base, rent a lot of movies.
RADIO VOICE. But not base, let's talk about Iraq. Did you see

a lot of action?

ELLIOT. Yeah.

RADIO VOICE. Were there times you were scared?

ELLIOT. The first time I heard a mortar shell. That scared the crap out of me. Literally.

RADIO VOICE. And you were injured. Tell me about that.

ELLIOT. It's a long story.

RADIO VOICE. What sticks out in your mind? About the experience?

ELLIOT. I got two corrective surgeries. They'll send me back if I want.

RADIO VOICE. To Iraq? Will you go?

ELLIOT. I mean, my leg is still messed up but. I'm not trying to stay here and work at Subway Hoagies. "Pardon me, sir, you want some hot peppers with that roast beef?"

RADIO VOICE. What do the troops think about politics? Do they support the war?

ELLIOT. Politics? Nobody cares about that. People drink their sorrows away. You hear people running down the hallway like, "F this!" "F that!" "Kill raghead!"

RADIO VOICE. (*Slightly changed tone.*) Editor flag last remark. (*Back to interview.*) Both your father and grandfather served in the military.

ELLIOT. My pop was in Vietnam, marine corps. Three purple hearts.

RADIO VOICE. It must be something else to trade war stories with your father.

ELLIOT. He doesn't bring up that stuff too much.

RADIO VOICE. Some say there's a code of silence after returning home.

ELLIOT. My mom's got a box of his old letters, his uniform, dog tags. Our basement flooded and everything is in piles down there. But I was like, mom you gotta find that stuff.

RADIO VOICE. What about your grandfather?

ELLIOT. He was in Korea. He was a flute player. He'll be like, "I played Mozart in the north when everyone had frostbite." He's got two or three stories that he just tells them over and over. He's got old-timers.

RADIO VOICE. Alzheimer's?

ELLIOT. Right.

RADIO VOICE. You must have felt a great deal of pressure to

enlist.

ELLIOT. Naw, I didn't even tell them. I just went one day and signed the papers.

RADIO VOICE. Just like that.

ELLIOT. Dad was actually kind of pissed, like, "The marines is no joke. The marines is going to mess with you."

RADIO VOICE. So why go then? *(No answer.)* Why did you enlist?

ELLIOT. I was like, dad was a marine. I want to be a marine. I really did it for him.

12/PRELUDE

The garden. Ginny holds a large yellow envelope stuffed full of papers. She pulls out one sheet at a time. Grandpop appears separately, reading a letter. Pop appears separately. He is incredibly happy, slightly drunk.

POP.
    April 4, '67
    To my pop back in the Bronx aka "Little P.R.,"
    The evac hospital was like Disney Land. Real beds.

GRANDPOP. Clean sheets.

POP. Fresh pajamas. The women there? I met this one nurse, Ginny. Nurse Ginny. So let me ask you.

GINNY. "Nurse Ginny."

POP. How old were you when you fell for mom?

GRANDPOP. Did you know right away she was your woman?

POP. I'm serious old man, I want answers. Got back to the platoon this morning. The guys were still alive, which is a good feeling. We had a big celebration.

GINNY. "Helmet stew."

POP. Hess' mom sent a package with wood alcohol. Stuff she made in the bathtub. Awful stuff.

GRANDPOP. We got drunk.

POP. Joe Bobb pulled out his guitar. I pulled out your flute. I made a big official speech, told them the whole story. You're a decorated veteran,

GINNY. "Bird watching."

POP. you served in Korea, back when they kept the Puerto Ricans separate. How you played the same exact flute to your platoon. Then when I enlisted you handed me the flute and said,

GRANDPOP. "You're a man. Teach yourself how to play."

POP. Joe Bobb showed me a hillbilly song. I showed him a danzón. The keys are sticking, it's the swamp. Low D won't budge, two of the pads fell off. Here's my little plan I'm putting together.

GRANDPOP. Get home safe.

POP. Marry nurse Ginny.

GINNY. "C-rations."

POP. Have a son, give him the flute. One flute, three generations. Aw man, right now Joe Bobb is throwing up all over. The smell is bad. It's the wood alcohol.

GRANDPOP. Tell mom my leg is okay.

GINNY. "Date unknown."

POP. And sorry I didn't write for so long.

13/PRELUDE

The garden, at night. Elliot stands in the garden. Pop's letters are on the ground.

ELLIOT. My little green Bible. Every soldier has something you take with you, no matter where you go, you take that thing. Waikiki had a tattoo of his mom. Mario had a gold cross his grandma had gave him. He wore it around his neck even though it was against the rules. I kept the Bible right inside my vest pocket. I had a picture of Stephanie in it, like a family portrait with all her cousins. My senior prom picture with all the guys. A picture of mom and pop. I looked at those pictures every day. Stared at those pictures. Daze off for like two hours at a time. *(Pause.)* The first guy I shot down, I kept his passport there.

One night, I don't know why, I was just going to kill my corporal. He was asleep. I put my rifle to the corporal's head and I was going to kill him. All I kept thinking was the bad stuff he made us do. He was the kind of guy who gets off on bringing down morale.

Like making us run with trench foot. Trench foot is when your feet start rotting. Because of chemical and biological weapons, we didn't take our boots off for thirty-six days straight. When I finally took my boots off, I had to peel my socks from the skin. They were black, and the second they came off, they became instantly hard. Corporal made us run with trench foot. Run to get the water. Run to get the ammo. Everyone was asleep and I was ready to pull the trigger. Waikiki woke up and saw what I was doing. He kicked my arm like, "Eh, man, let's switch." So I looked at my pictures and slept, he went on watch. The next day me and Waikiki were running to get the water and he was like, "Eh, man, what were you doing last night?" I was like, "I don't know." He was like, "It's alright. We'll be out of here soon."

After I got injured, when my chopper landed in Spain. They pulled me out of there. They cut. My clothes were so disgusting they had to cut them off my body. My underwear was so black. The nurse had to cut it up the sides and take it off me like a pamper. The second she did that, it turned hard like a cast of plaster. You could see the shape of everything. Everything. It looked like an invisible man was wearing them. She threw it like a basketball in the trash. When the guys had finally found me, they had stuffed my leg full of cotton rags. The nurse counted one two three then ripped all the cotton out. I thought I was gonna die. I broke the metal railing right off the stretcher.

They didn't have underwear to put on me so they put a hospital gown instead. The kind that opens in the back and you can see the butt. I was still on the runway. The chopper took off, my gown flew up over my face, but my hands were tied down so I couldn't do nothing. I was butt naked in the middle of everybody. Next thing I know, someone pulled the gown away from my face and I saw this fine female looking down at me. When I saw her, it was like angels singing. *(He imitates angels singing.)* Like, *aaaaaaah.* So what's the first thing that's gonna happen to a guy? She saw it. I was so embarrassed.

The sponge baths I got while I was over there? They give you a sponge bath every other day. The first time. Once again, it was another fine female. It was four months since I seen one. Most female officers, out in the field, they don't look like this one did. So something happened, you know what happened. She was sponging me down and saw it and was like, "You want me to leave the room?" After three days she got used to it. She would be chatting, changing the subject. When you catch a woody with an officer, who you have to see everyday in Spain? The day I left she was like, "Yo, take care of your friend."

When I first landed in Philly Chucky and Buckwheat met me at the airport. They came running up to the gate like, "Did you kill em? Did you kill em? Did you have a gun? Did you have a really big gun?" I was like, nah, don't you worry about none of that. Don't think about those things. I was trying to forget, but that's how they see me now. That's what I am. That's how Stephanie sees me. And the guys.

On the airplane flying home. All I could think was, I have to talk to pop. Hear his stories. He used to tell stuff from the war but looking back, it was mostly jokes. Like he swallowed a thing of chewing tobacco and puked for three days. He took a leak off a tank and a pretty Vietnamese lady saw him. He never sat me down and told me what it was like, for real. The first night I got here, I was like, pop, I need to hear it from your mouth. That was Monday. He was like, we'll talk about it Tuesday. Wednesday rolled around, I'm like, pop I'm only home a week. Did you have nightmares, too? Every single night? Did you feel guilty, too? When you shot a guy? Things he never opened up about. Finally I got him real drunk, I'm like, now's the time. I was like, did you shoot anyone up close? Did you shoot a civilian? Anything. He threw the table at me. Threw his beer bottle on the steps. Marched up the stairs, slammed the door.

Seeing mom, it takes so much stress off. She laid me down, and worked on my leg in an old-fashioned way. Went to the herb store, got all her magic potions. The gauze bandage, it hardly came off. I could peel it back like a inch. The rest was infected, stuck to the gauze. At night, it itched so bad I had to scream. Mom laid me down in her garden, she told me to relax. Breathe in. Breathe out. Breathe like a circle. She told me to close my eyes and imagine the time I was happiest in my entire life. Then I felt her fingers on my leg. That felt so good. Hands that love you touching your worst place. I started to cry like a baby. I don't know why. It's just, I forgot how that feels. Like home. The tears were just coming. She put aloe and all sorts of stuff in there. I could tell she was crying too. She knows I been through a lot. She understands. *(Ginny enters. She begins to braid vines around Elliot's body, from the garden. She wraps his body in intricate, meticulous ways. She adds leaves and other flora. This is a slow process. It lasts until the end of the scene.)*

35

It's a hard question. Of every second in your life, nail down the best one. I started playing memories, like a movie in my mind. The prom. Me all slicked out with the guys, in our silver suits. Matching silver shoes. Hooking up with Stephanie. All the different places me and Steph got freaky. In her mom's house. On top of the roof for New Year's. This one time I took Sean fishing down the Allegheny. He farted real loud. He ripped a nasty one. All the white dudes, in their fisherman hats, they were like, "Crazy Puerto Ricans. You scared the fish away."

The first time I ever went to Puerto Rico. With mom and pop. We drove around the island with the windows rolled down. I was like, damn, so this is where I come from. This is my roots. This one time we stopped at Luquillo beach. The water was light light blue, and flat like a table, no waves. Mom was like, "Pull over, George, and teach me to swim." We swam in there like for five hours. Pop was holding mom on the surface of the water. He would hold on, like, "You ready? You ready?" She was like, "Ay! Hold on, papi! I'm gonna sink!" And he would let go and she would stay, floating, on the top. She was so happy. It looked like they were in love. Then you could see the moon in the water. It was still day but she floated on the moon. I could live in that day forever. See them like that every day.

After mom fixed my leg, she was like, "I got a gift for you. Something important." She gave me a fat yellow envelope. Crusty and old. She was like, "Burn this or read it. It's up to you." I sat out in the garden, started pulling letters out of the envelope. It was all of pop's letters from Vietnam. *(Pop enters the garden.)*

POP. Date unknown

ELLIOT. I read every one. All night, I didn't hardly move.

POP.
Dad,
I just want to say I'm sorry.

ELLIOT. I was like, pop, I fucking walked in your shoes.

POP. I threw your flute away.

ELLIOT. Pop, we lived the same fucking life.

POP. All these thoughts were going through my head like thinking about the Bronx, you, mom.

ELLIOT. It's scary how much was the same. Killing a guy. Getting your leg scratched up. Falling in love.

POP. They got Hess and Joe Bobb.

ELLIOT. Nightmares. Meds. Infections. Letters to your father.

POP. One instant. Their bodies were covered with dust. Tree bark.

Their eyes.

ELLIOT. Even ripping them up, taping them back together. It was like the feeling from Puerto Rico, but not a peaceful feeling.

POP. It was like shoot someone, destroy something. I threw your flute in the river.

ELLIOT. You see all the shit you can't erase. Like, here's who you are, Elliot, and you never even knew.

POP. You can't sit around and feel sorry for yourself or you're gonna die. I had to do something, so that's what I did. *(Pop's letter is done.)*

ELLIOT. Pop's up on the second floor, got the AC on, watching TV. Probably smoking weed. Probably doesn't even know I seen his letters. I know he won't even come to the airport tomorrow. He'll just be like: *(Pop speaks directly to Elliot.)*

POP. Well, you chose it so good luck with it. Don't do anything stupid. *(Elliot is tangled in vines. Lights fade.)*

14/FUGUE

The empty space. Three duffel bags are on the floor.

GINNY.
    A runway.
    The Philadelphia airport tarmac.
    July 2003 is dry and windy.
    Two seagulls fly even though the ocean is miles away.
    Luggage carts roll in one direction,
    Taxiing planes in another.
    The windows are sealed to airtight, noisetight.
    People crowd around the departure monitors.
ELLIOT.
    A man enters.
(Elliot enters.)
    Cologne is sprayed on his neck.
    A clean shave.
(Elliot looks at his watch.)
    0700 hours.
    Thinking in military time again.

He fixes his short hair.
(Elliot fixes his short hair.)
    Grabs his life.
(Elliot picks up a duffel bag.)
    Inside his bag are two fatigues his mother ironed this morning.
    Fresh sorullito from grandmom.
    Still warm, wrapped in two paper towels.
    Grease-sealed in a plastic bag.
    A naked photo from Stephanie.
    In the photo she is smiling and holding in her stomach.
    Her skin is brown.
    The hair on her body is brown.
    She is blinking, her eyes half closed.
GINNY.
    San Juan Bay.
    A boarding ramp.
    A transport ship to South Korea
    Via Japan via Panama Canal.
    September 1950 is mild.
    The water is light light blue.
    And flat like a table, no waves.
GRANDPOP.
    A boy enters.
(Grandpop enters. He stands beside Elliot and picks up another duffel bag. Grandpop waves goodbye to his family, offstage.)
    Slacks pressed.
    Hair combed.
    Family standing at the rails.
    His wife wears a cotton dress.
    Sweat gathers in her brown curls.
    On her hip, Little George.
    His five year old son.
    A boarding ramp.
    Corrugated steel.
    His first ride on the ocean.
(Grandpop picks up his duffel and freezes.)
GINNY.
    A runway.
    The Newark Airport tarmac.
    August 1965 is unseasonably cool.
(Pop enters. He stands beside Elliot and picks up a duffel bag.)

POP.

A boy enters.

(He looks at his watch.)

9:15 A.M.

He will never get used to military time.

He grabs his life.

At the bottom of his duffel, good luck charms.

A red handball glove.

A bottle of vodka from the Social Sevens.

Two pencils and paper.

A long corridor.

A gray carpeted ramp.

A plane to Parris Island

To a ship to Vietnam.

(Pop picks up his duffel and freezes.)

ELLIOT.

The bag

The duffel

The photo

Stephanie

Teeth

Jazz

Calvin Klein

Fubu

Flute

Helmet

Thirty-six springs

Ink

Heliconia

Handwriting

(Elliot grabs his duffel, steps forward.)

He walks down the gray carpeted ramp.

Boards the plane to Camp Pendleton.

Where he will board his second ship to Kuwait.

Where he will cross the border north into Iraq.

Again.

Happy he has an aisle seat.

Going back to war.

End of Play

PROPERTY LIST

Man's white undershorts
Towel
Marine uniform — Iraq War
Marine cavalry uniform — Vietnam War
Boots, socks
Undershirt
Paper, pencil, envelope
3 duffel bags
Little green Bible with four photos
Walkman and headphones
Heavy army uniform — Korean War
Additional clothes for warmth
Black leather case for flute
Flute in pieces
Heliconia leaf
2 wallets with 2 photos in each
Night vision goggles
Binoculars
TV mike on shirt collar
Strip of cloth for tourniquet
Pack of cigarettes
A joint to smoke
Large radio station headphones
Large yellow envelope stuffed with letters

NEW PLAYS

★ **GUARDIANS by Peter Morris.** In this unflinching look at war, a disgraced American soldier discloses the truth about Abu Ghraib prison, and a clever English journalist reveals how he faked a similar story for the London tabloids. "Compelling, sympathetic and powerful." *–NY Times.* "Sends you into a state of moral turbulence." *–Sunday Times (UK).* "Nothing short of remarkable." *–Village Voice.* [1M, 1W] ISBN: 978-0-8222-2177-7

★ **BLUE DOOR by Tanya Barfield.** Three generations of men (all played by one actor), from slavery through Black Power, challenge Lewis, a tenured professor of mathematics, to embark on a journey combining past and present. "A teasing flare for words." *–Village Voice.* "Unfailingly thought-provoking." *–LA Times.* "The play moves with the speed and logic of a dream." *–Seattle Weekly.* [2M] ISBN: 978-0-8222-2209-5

★ **THE INTELLIGENT DESIGN OF JENNY CHOW by Rolin Jones.** This irreverent "techno-comedy" chronicles one brilliant woman's quest to determine her heritage and face her fears with the help of her astounding creation called Jenny Chow. "Boldly imagined." *–NY Times.* "Fantastical and funny." *–Variety.* "Harvests many laughs and finally a few tears." *–LA Times.* [3M, 3W] ISBN: 978-0-8222-2071-8

★ **SOUVENIR by Stephen Temperley.** Florence Foster Jenkins, a wealthy society eccentric, suffers under the delusion that she is a great coloratura soprano—when in fact the opposite is true. "Hilarious and deeply touching. Incredibly moving and breathtaking." *–NY Daily News.* "A sweet love letter of a play." *–NY Times.* "Wildly funny. Completely charming." *–Star-Ledger.* [1M, 1W] ISBN: 978-0-8222-2157-9

★ **ICE GLEN by Joan Ackermann.** In this touching period comedy, a beautiful poetess dwells in idyllic obscurity on a Berkshire estate with a band of unlikely cohorts. "A beautifully written story of nature and change." *–Talkin' Broadway.* "A lovely play which will leave you with a lot to think about." *–CurtainUp.* "Funny, moving and witty." *–Metroland (Boston).* [4M, 3W] ISBN: 978-0-8222-2175-3

★ **THE LAST DAYS OF JUDAS ISCARIOT by Stephen Adly Guirgis.** Set in a time-bending, darkly comic world between heaven and hell, this play reexamines the plight and fate of the New Testament's most infamous sinner. "An unforced eloquence that finds the poetry in lowdown street talk." *–NY Times.* "A real jaw-dropper." *–Variety.* "An extraordinary play." *–Guardian (UK).* [10M, 5W] ISBN: 978-0-8222-2082-4

DRAMATISTS PLAY SERVICE, INC.
440 Park Avenue South, New York, NY 10016 212-683-8960 Fax 212-213-1539
postmaster@dramatists.com   www.dramatists.com

NEW PLAYS

★ **THE GREAT AMERICAN TRAILER PARK MUSICAL music and lyrics by David Nehls, book by Betsy Kelso.** Pippi, a stripper on the run, has just moved into Armadillo Acres, wreaking havoc among the tenants of Florida's most exclusive trailer park. "Adultery, strippers, murderous ex-boyfriends, Costco and the Ice Capades. Undeniable fun." —*NY Post.* "Joyful and unashamedly vulgar." —*The New Yorker.* "Sparkles with treasure." —*New York Sun.* [2M, 5W] ISBN: 978-0-8222-2137-1

★ **MATCH by Stephen Belber.** When a young Seattle couple meet a prominent New York choreographer, they are led on a fraught journey that will change their lives forever. "Uproariously funny, deeply moving, enthralling theatre." —*NY Daily News.* "Prolific laughs and ear-to-ear smiles." —*NY Magazine.* [2M, 1W] ISBN: 978-0-8222-2020-6

★ **MR. MARMALADE by Noah Haidle.** Four-year-old Lucy's imaginary friend, Mr. Marmalade, doesn't have much time for her—not to mention he has a cocaine addiction and a penchant for pornography. "Alternately hilarious and heartbreaking." —*The New Yorker.* "A mature and accomplished play." —*LA Times.* "Scathingly observant comedy." —*Miami Herald.* [4M, 2W] ISBN: 978-0-8222-2142-5

★ **MOONLIGHT AND MAGNOLIAS by Ron Hutchinson.** Three men cloister themselves as they work tirelessly to reshape a screenplay that's just not working—*Gone with the Wind.* "Consumers of vintage Hollywood insider stories will eat up Hutchinson's diverting conjecture." —*Variety.* "A lot of fun." —*NY Post.* "A Hollywood dream-factory farce." —*Chicago Sun-Times.* [3M, 1W] ISBN: 978-0-8222-2084-8

★ **THE LEARNED LADIES OF PARK AVENUE by David Grimm, translated and freely adapted from Molière's *Les Femmes Savantes.*** Dicky wants to marry Betty, but her mother's plan is for Betty to wed a most pompous man. "A brave, brainy and barmy revision." —*Hartford Courant.* "A rare but welcome bird in contemporary theatre." —*New Haven Register.* "Roll over Cole Porter." —*Boston Globe.* [5M, 5W] ISBN: 978-0-8222-2135-7

★ **REGRETS ONLY by Paul Rudnick.** A sparkling comedy of Manhattan manners that explores the latest topics in marriage, friendships and squandered riches. "One of the funniest quip-meisters on the planet." —*NY Times.* "Precious moments of hilarity. Devastatingly accurate political and social satire." —*BackStage.* "Great fun." —*CurtainUp.* [3M, 3W] ISBN: 978-0-8222-2223-1

DRAMATISTS PLAY SERVICE, INC.
440 Park Avenue South, New York, NY 10016 212-683-8960 Fax 212-213-1539
postmaster@dramatists.com www.dramatists.com

NEW PLAYS

★ **AFTER ASHLEY by Gina Gionfriddo.** A teenager is unwillingly thrust into the national spotlight when a family tragedy becomes talk-show fodder. "A work that virtually any audience would find accessible." *—NY Times.* "Deft characterization and caustic humor." *—NY Sun.* "A smart satirical drama." *—Variety.* [4M, 2W] ISBN: 978-0-8222-2099-2

★ **THE RUBY SUNRISE by Rinne Groff.** Twenty-five years after Ruby struggles to realize her dream of inventing the first television, her daughter faces similar battles of faith as she works to get Ruby's story told on network TV. "Measured and intelligent, optimistic yet clear-eyed." *—NY Magazine.* "Maintains an exciting sense of ingenuity." *—Village Voice.* "Sinuous theatrical flair." *—Broadway.com.* [3M, 4W] ISBN: 978-0-8222-2140-1

★ **MY NAME IS RACHEL CORRIE taken from the writings of Rachel Corrie, edited by Alan Rickman and Katharine Viner.** This solo piece tells the story of Rachel Corrie who was killed in Gaza by an Israeli bulldozer set to demolish a Palestinian home. "Heartbreaking urgency. An invigoratingly detailed portrait of a passionate idealist." *—NY Times.* "Deeply authentically human." *—USA Today.* "A stunning dramatization." *—CurtainUp.* [1W] ISBN: 978-0-8222-2222-4

★ **ALMOST, MAINE by John Cariani.** This charming midwinter night's dream of a play turns romantic clichés on their ear as it chronicles the painfully hilarious amorous adventures (and misadventures) of residents of a remote northern town that doesn't quite exist. "A whimsical approach to the joys and perils of romance." *—NY Times.* "Sweet, poignant and witty." *—NY Daily News.* "Aims for the heart by way of the funny bone." *—Star-Ledger.* [2M, 2W] ISBN: 978-0-8222-2156-2

★ **Mitch Albom's TUESDAYS WITH MORRIE by Jeffrey Hatcher and Mitch Albom, based on the book by Mitch Albom.** The true story of Brandeis University professor Morrie Schwartz and his relationship with his student Mitch Albom. "A touching, life-affirming, deeply emotional drama." *—NY Daily News.* "You'll laugh. You'll cry." *—Variety.* "Moving and powerful." *—NY Post.* [2M] ISBN: 978-0-8222-2188-3

★ **DOG SEES GOD: CONFESSIONS OF A TEENAGE BLOCKHEAD by Bert V. Royal.** An abused pianist and a pyromaniac ex-girlfriend contribute to the teen-angst of America's most hapless kid. "A welcome antidote to the notion that the *Peanuts* gang provides merely American cuteness." *—NY Times.* "Hysterically funny." *—NY Post.* "The *Peanuts* kids have finally come out of their shells." *—Time Out.* [4M, 4W] ISBN: 978-0-8222-2152-4

DRAMATISTS PLAY SERVICE, INC.
440 Park Avenue South, New York, NY 10016 212-683-8960 Fax 212-213-1539
postmaster@dramatists.com   www.dramatists.com

NEW PLAYS

★ **RABBIT HOLE by David Lindsay-Abaire.** Winner of the 2007 Pulitzer Prize. Becca and Howie Corbett have everything a couple could want until a life-shattering accident turns their world upside down. "An intensely emotional examination of grief, laced with wit." —*Variety.* "A transcendent and deeply affecting new play." —*Entertainment Weekly.* "Painstakingly beautiful." —*BackStage.* [2M, 3W] ISBN: 978-0-8222-2154-8

★ **DOUBT, A Parable by John Patrick Shanley.** Winner of the 2005 Pulitzer Prize and Tony Award. Sister Aloysius, a Bronx school principal, takes matters into her own hands when she suspects the young Father Flynn of improper relations with one of the male students. "All the elements come invigoratingly together like clockwork." —*Variety.* "Passionate, exquisite, important, engrossing." —*NY Newsday.* [1M, 3W] ISBN: 978-0-8222-2219-4

★ **THE PILLOWMAN by Martin McDonagh.** In an unnamed totalitarian state, an author of horrific children's stories discovers that someone has been making his stories come true. "A blindingly bright black comedy." —*NY Times.* "McDonagh's least forgiving, bravest play." —*Variety.* "Thoroughly startling and genuinely intimidating." —*Chicago Tribune.* [4M, 5 bit parts (2M, 1W, 1 boy, 1 girl)] ISBN: 978-0-8222-2100-5

★ **GREY GARDENS book by Doug Wright, music by Scott Frankel, lyrics by Michael Korie.** The hilarious and heartbreaking story of Big Edie and Little Edie Bouvier Beale, the eccentric aunt and cousin of Jacqueline Kennedy Onassis, once bright names on the social register who became East Hampton's most notorious recluses. "An experience no passionate theatergoer should miss." —*NY Times.* "A unique and unmissable musical." —*Rolling Stone.* [4M, 3W, 2 girls] ISBN: 978-0-8222-2181-4

★ **THE LITTLE DOG LAUGHED by Douglas Carter Beane.** Mitchell Green could make it big as the hot new leading man in Hollywood if Diane, his agent, could just keep him in the closet. "Devastatingly funny." —*NY Times.* "An out-and-out delight." —*NY Daily News.* "Full of wit and wisdom." —*NY Post.* [2M, 2W] ISBN: 978-0-8222-2226-2

★ **SHINING CITY by Conor McPherson.** A guilt-ridden man reaches out to a therapist after seeing the ghost of his recently deceased wife. "Haunting, inspired and glorious." —*NY Times.* "Simply breathtaking and astonishing." —*Time Out.* "A thoughtful, artful, absorbing new drama." —*Star-Ledger.* [3M, 1W] ISBN: 978-0-8222-2187-6

DRAMATISTS PLAY SERVICE, INC.
440 Park Avenue South, New York, NY 10016 212-683-8960 Fax 212-213-1539
postmaster@dramatists.com   www.dramatists.com